Roundy & Friends
Russia

Special Edition

Andres Varela

Illustrations and Graphic Design by Carlos F. González
Co-Producer Germán Hernández
Second Edition
© 2019 Soccertowns® LLC

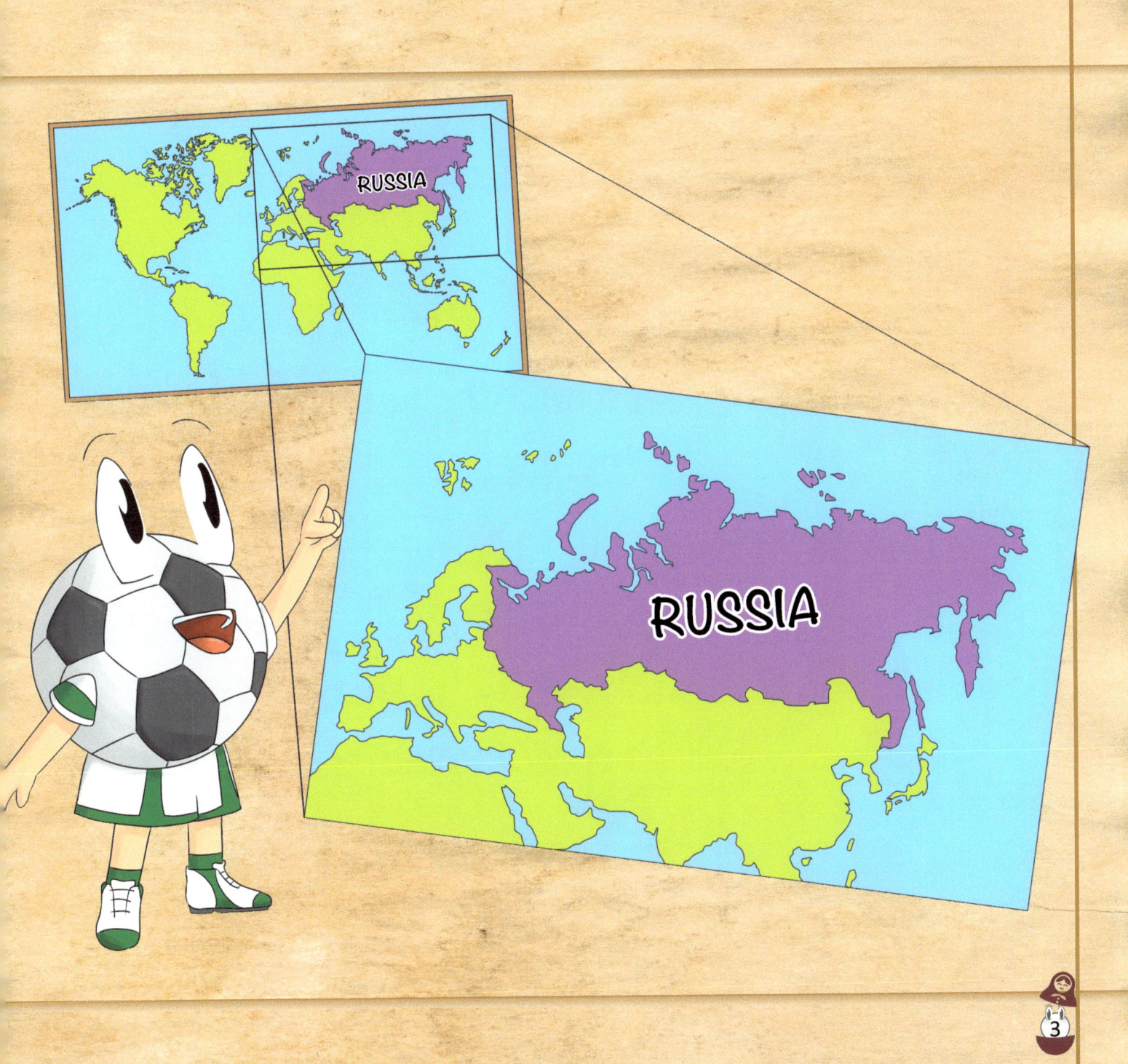

Russia is the largest country in the world and the ninth most populated country with 144 Million people!

Teo planned a route over 11 cities hosting a World Championship. The team will travel by train between the cities. The first stop will be Sochi and the last one will be Kaliningrad.

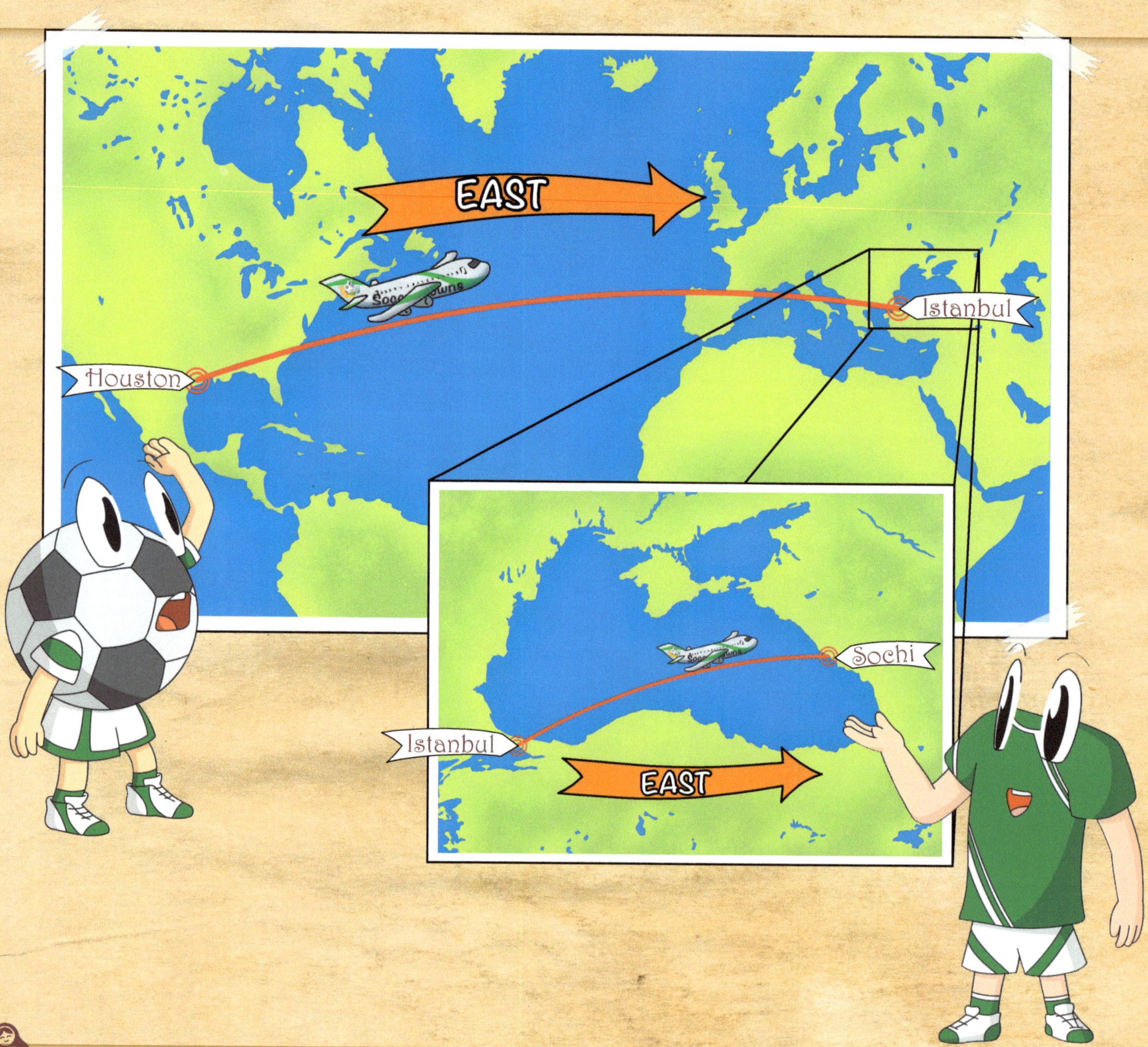
EAST
Istanbul
Houston
Sochi
Istanbul
EAST

They take a plane from Houston, Texas to Istanbul, Turkey which takes 12 hours! After a short layover, they fly over the Black Sea for 1 hour and 35 minutes to Sochi.

As the plane landed, Teo told the team some interesting facts about Sochi. Sochi is Russia's largest resort city with a permanent population of over 430,000 people. The city hosted the 2014 winter Olympics.

The Port of Sochi was improved in 2013 in order to accommodate large tourist boat cruises.

Fisht Olympic Stadium was also built in 2013 and it can hold 47,000 soccer fans during the championship.

The Sochi Arboretum contains a unique collection of subtropical flora and fauna.

Fisht Olympic Stadium

Sochi Arboretum

Port of Sochi

Winter sports

The group decides to spend a day at the beach where they meet hundreds of soccer fans ready to watch some quality soccer matches over the next few days.

The following afternoon they are excited as they enter Fisht Stadium to watch a great game - the current world champions Germany vs. Sweden!

Fisht Olympic Stadium

After watching an amazing game, they take an overnight train to the next destination: Rostov-on-Don.

They get to sleep comfortably in the train as it chugs North for approximately 8 hours.

Rostov-on-Don is a port city on the Don River. The population is approximately 1,090,000 people.

Located really close to the Don River and built in 2017, The Rostov Arena has capacity for 45,000 soccer fans. It will host several games from the Championship. The group got tickets for the match between Iceland vs. Croatia. Roundy is very excited as he's heard the Iceland fans are so much fun!

The next destination is Volgograd. They take the train ride for nine and a half hours.

The group doesn't have tickets to a game in Volgograd so they visit the city, participating in a Fan Festival, which the Russian government helps organize to allow soccer fans to watch games on very large screens.

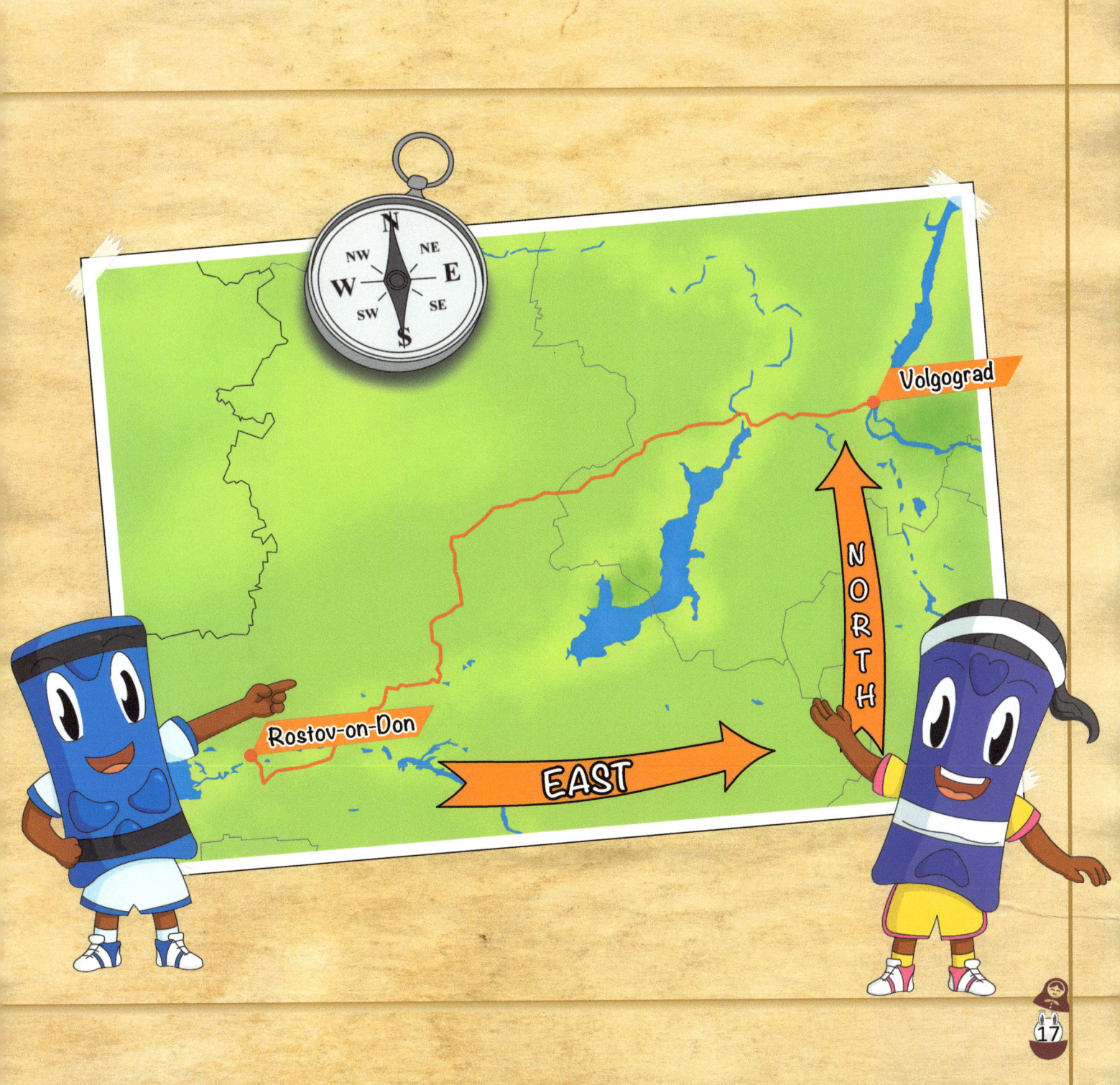

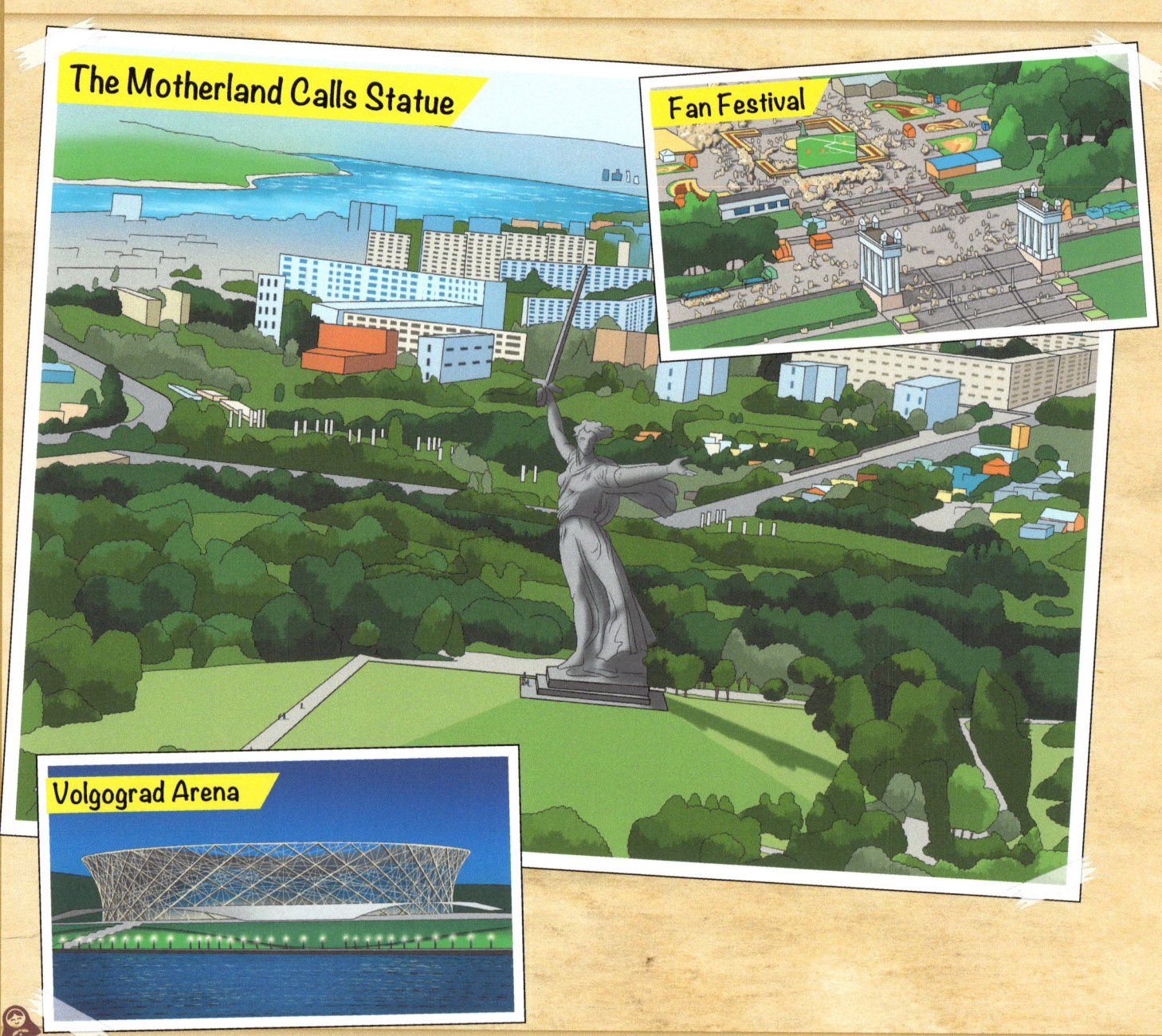

The city is situated on the Western Bank of the Volga River. The population is approximately 1,021,000 people. The city was called Tsaritsyn prior to 1925, renamed Stalingrad until 1961, when it was renamed again as Volgograd which translates "Volga City".

The Motherland Calls Statue is the tallest statue of a woman in the world. "Wow, that's even bigger than the Statue of Liberty," says Roundy! "It was built in 1967 and it is dedicated to the 'Heroes of the Battle of Stalingrad' from World War II when the Russian army defended the city against invaders from other countries," Teo explained.

The Volgograd Arena has a capacity of 45,500 fans.

Leaving Volgograd, they travel by train for over 16 hours to reach Samara.

The city is located where the Volga River and the Samara River meet.

Samara has a population of approximately 1,170,000 people.

The train station where they arrive is very modern. Displaying over 900 aerospace history exhibits, the Cosmic Samara Museum opened in 2007. The team makes a quick visit to the museum, learning that during World War II Samara built more than 27,000 of the war aircraft IL-2, which became a symbol of Soviet force in those days.

The group then enjoys playing a nice beach soccer game before heading to the stadium.

At the Stadium they will watch the game between Colombia vs. Senegal.

After watching an exciting game in Samara, they head Northeast over to Yekaterinburg. It's a 13 hour train ride.

The city has a population of over 1,480,000 people and it is located along the Iset River.

They couldn't find tickets to a match as they were sold out, so they decided to visit some touristic attractions.

The city was named after Russian Emperor Peter the Great's wife, Yekaterina.

At the time it was a strategic connection between Europe and Asia and it became the mining capital of the Russian Empire.

From Yekaterinburg they head West to Kazan

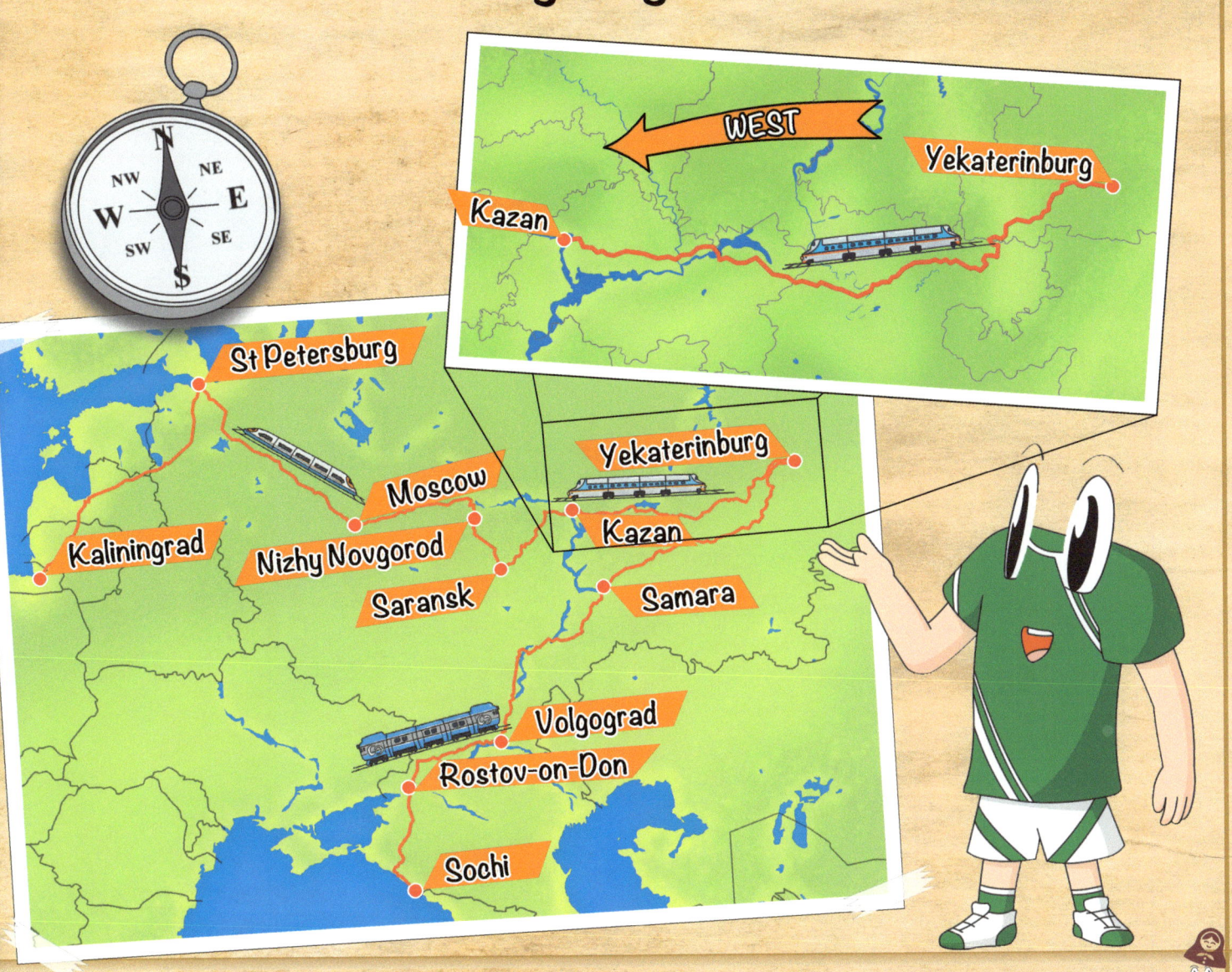

Kazan is known as the sports capital of Russia. They visit some of the sports complexes used for major events in the past.

Kazan will host the Quaterfinal game of the championship in a few days. Jersey explains "Quaterfinal" means there are 8 teams divided in four matches.

We had some much fun touring many cities in Russia! Come and see us back in the next special edition, we still have many other places to show you!

Next stop is Saransk! A six hour train ride from Kazan.

www.ingramcontent.com/pod-product-compliance
Lightning Source LLC
Chambersburg PA
CBHW041502220426
43661CB00016B/1231